London Living Style

TEXT BY
Lesley Astaire

PHOTOGRAPHS BY
Michael Boys

RIZZOLI
NEW YORK

TO

Monty and Sheila Berman
Jenny Green
Suzanne Slesin

First published in the United States of America in 1990 by
Rizzoli International Publications, Inc.
300 Park Avenue South, New York, NY 10010

Text copyright © 1990 Thames and Hudson Ltd, London
Photographs copyright © 1990 Michael Boys

Library of Congress Cataloging-in-Publication Data

Astaire, Lesley
London living style / by Lesley Astaire; photographs by Michael Boys.
p.   cm.
ISBN 0-8478-1280-4
1. Interior decoration—England—London—Themes, motives.
I. Title.
NK2044.L6A88 1990
747.22' 1—dc20   *90–53108*
CIP

Printed and bound in West Germany

Contents

Introduction

From the arrival of the Romans 2,000 years ago to the twentieth-century refugees from Hitler's Germany and West Indians seeking a livelihood, London has been a place dominated by visitors and settlers who were not born there. Like myself (who arrived from Newcastle-upon-Tyne nearly thirty years ago), those who did not first see the light of day within sound of "Bow bells", as the authentic Cockney should do, seem to feel perfectly at home here – and largely because London is valued above all as a most "livable" city.

It could well be that the very tides of change in the inhabitants that flow over the city contribute most to its livability, for – unlike any other great

Western city – London has never been planned at any age. Unlike New York and most other important American cities, it has very few gridiron street schemes; unlike Paris, no emperor and his town-planner have had a large-scale impact on the layout; no single period dominates London's buildings as Ancient Rome still dominates its modern-day descendant. Rather than being planned, London has grown from many centres like an organic growth. Scratch the surface of any part of London and layers of history reveal themselves – mainly as a result of this organic growth, but also because of the lack of any kind of wide-sweeping change. Hitler's bombs and the Great Fire of 1666 were the only major incidents in London's 2,000 years of peaceful development.

The description of London as a collection of villages joined together is well known; indeed there are guide books which explore the particular delights of the likes of Hampstead and Highgate to the north, Bermondsey and Poplar to the east, Paddington and Chelsea to the west, and Lambeth and Wandsworth to the south. Each of these and many other parts of the body of London do have, and have had for many centuries, their equivalent of the village green, parish church, town hall and "High Street".

But the best way to grasp the complex maze that is London is to recognize that at the centre of these villages are the two long-established Cities: Westminster and the City of London. Situated little more than two miles apart, they stand at each end of the outer edge of a long arc of the River Thames, which faces due south and has a deep-water channel providing excellent access for river transport. Along this bend and between the two Cities once stood great palaces, with one front door to the river and one front door to the great road that runs along the full length from Westminster Abbey and Parliament at one end – down Whitehall, the Strand (a name derived from the river bank), Fleet Street (where the old Fleet River meets the Thames), skirting around St Paul's down Upper and Lower Thames Street – to the Tower at the other end. The remnants of the river-bank palaces are frequently still there in one form or another: the Palace of Westminster at one end along with the great official and government buildings along Whitehall, Charing Cross Station on the site of Hungerford House, the Savoy Hotel where the Savoy Palace was, the surviving Temple and Inns of Court. In the City, however, many of the great trading palaces and warehouses have gone, except for Billingsgate (now fish-less but filled with hi-tech office space). And finally there is the Tower itself, Mecca for tourists from all parts of the globe.

To live in Westminster or the City is not only still possible, it is considered most desirable. Residential squares and terraces of houses are still the main feature of Westminster, and in the City the Corporation's ambitious housing scheme at the Barbican provides a major residential district. City fringes like Spitalfields have become some of the most unspoilt and historic residential streets anywhere in London.

However, it is in the accretion of "village" centres that most Londoners live, since the two Cities are by and large for the very rich. Most of these "villages" grew up in the countryside surrounding the older centres, particularly along the tributary rivers, which gave names and identity to various neighbour-hoods as well as winding street layouts along their way. The Westbourne River passes through Paddington and lends its name to the wide avenue planned and laid out in Victorian times; it was dammed to form the lake called Serpentine, the focus of all the landscaping in Hyde Park; and further south it runs through the old centre of Chelsea. Around Hyde Park are some of the most elegant and valued residential areas of London – Kensington, Knights-bridge, Belgravia, Mayfair and Bayswater.

The Rivers Tyburn and Fleet come down from Hampstead and Highgate, and along their courses are St John's Wood and Marylebone (under Marylebone High Street lies the Tyburn in a great sewer). The dammed Tyburn forms a popular lake for Regent's Park and around Regent's Park are, again, some of the finest residential areas, including the Nash Terraces. The river continues further south through Mayfair and Pimlico. And south of the Thames such rivers as the Wandle, the Effra and the Ravensbourne have had similar roles to play in the history of London.

I have to confess that I know much less about South London, and I am aware that, for many Londoners, the Thames is a significant north/south divide. The south is different from the other side, and in particular it has no dominating centre like Westminster or the City. It has always been an ideal place of gardens and entertainment along its banks – from the Elizabethan Globe Theatre (it had the good fortune to lie outside the City's curfew bound-aries), which sat among alehouses, bath-houses and bearbaiting pits, to Victo-rian pleasure parks like Belvedere Gardens opposite the Savoy, Vauxhall Gardens opposite where the Tate Gallery now stands, and to the present century when riverside parks run from the Greenwich peninsula to Battersea Park, Kew Gardens, Richmond and beyond. In South London the countryside seems much closer, or rather its residential character is more rural than that of the urban north, with fine and venerable places like Dulwich, Putney, Kew and Richmond having more than their share of Georgian houses and Victorian villas set in long, low-density sprawl with plenty of trees and old pubs.

This layering of historical patterns explains much of London as it is today. In the south the railways bringing commuters to the City and the West End had to cut their devastating way right through residential areas in order to deposit their passengers across the river, whereas those in the north were merely carrying goods into the city (coal, iron, foodstuffs) and built their termini along an outer ring. The fine stations of Paddington, Euston, St Pancras, Kings Cross and Liverpool Street all kept their distance from the centre along good distribution routes such as the early "ring road" of Marylebone Road and the Regent's Canal, which links all the stations to London's docks. North London commuters were also provided with the world's first underground railway to get them to work, an invisible system that made it possible to keep the fabric of London above ground more or less intact. In addition, the underground system was well designed and its stations, some of them minor masterpieces, were instrumental in creating new "villages" or reinforcing old ones.

The house I have lived in for fifteen years is in Maida Vale, itself a product of the Bakerloo underground line, which at this point follows the old Roman road of Watling Street to Edgware and beyond. I like to think that I have converted and altered bits of my house in a spirit akin to that of London itself – in the strong belief that the *ad hoc* and pragmatic can achieve a particular kind of harmony. London is a web of virtuoso bits, which add up to create a unique and wonderfully livable city without grand gestures.

TERRY FARRELL

Terry Farrell's house
in Maida Vale.

Overleaf, Maida Vale, a broad
avenue which gives its name to
an entire area, is one of the main
arteries that leads traffic out of
London to the north. Once
associated with artists' studios
and a rather bohemian way of
life, it has altered its character
since the turn of the century and
is now known mainly for the
massive apartment buildings,
offering roomy family flats, that
were built along both sides of the
road beginning around 1890.
They are in various architectural
styles, including this massive
example of mock-Tudor half-
timbering.

A Villa and a Garden

he site on which this St John's Wood villa was built in the 1820s was originally an orchard. There is still an old, old apple tree in the garden which lives quite happily with the almost jungle-like profusion of bushes, shrubs and even the odd palm tree.

The house has grown with its owners and is full of intriguing passages with rooms on different levels; for example, a small study on the upper floor is approached from outside by a spiral staircase.

With its large private garden and its swimming pool, one could imagine on a warm sunny day that one was in the South of France.

A view towards the drawing room from the hall with its antique wall hangings and traditional wallpaper.

Right above, a painting by Ivon Hitchens hangs above an antique daybed. The wall covering is a silk straw from the 1960s.

Right below, a collection of buckles is artfully arranged in a painted coffee table. The lithograph above the Chinese chest is by Bridget Riley.

Opposite, a general view of the imposing drawing room whose charm is achieved through the combination of an eclectic range of furniture and contemporary pictures.

The dining room has a floor of Italian tiles and the walls
are covered with silver foil paper. The chairs are English
Regency.

A bust of Bernard Shaw by Sir Jacob Epstein.

The owners of this unusual garden grow their plants in old receptacles.

Looking from the drawing room into the lush, mature garden and the pool.

Small Is Beautiful

*O*ne is greeted by a flat-fronted Georgian façade in a Chelsea street well-known for its architectural variety. The house is only twelve feet wide, but it is cleverly designed to create a real sense of space, even grandeur. The dining room/library has a mirrored inset on a domed ceiling, and the room is lined with mahogany. There are two charming double bedrooms with hand-printed wallpapers, and the bathrooms, with their use of both real and faux marble, are handsome and well-equipped.

Above right, a view into the dining room from the miniature hallway.

On the dining room shelves, Chinese pots and vases alternate with books.

This elaborate French clock belonged to the former owners of the house.

Opposite, the dining room/library has English chairs with slip covers. Above the bookshelves around the room is a collection of blue and white pots. The small mirrored dome in the ceiling adds a theatrical and, at the same time, cosy effect.

The mantelshelf in the drawing room. The two heads are by John Davies.

Opposite, Sammy, adopted from the Battersea pound, sits in the most comfortable chair in the upstairs studio/sitting room. For a small house, the height of the room is exceptional, and the pictures are hung on old brass gallery rods.

The studio/drawing-room, which in the past housed exhibitions of up and coming painters, now has a collection of the owners' own art. The atmosphere of the house is enhanced by the unusual use of colour throughout.
Every part of this dwelling is well used, every door hides a storage cupboard or a minuscule kitchen – truly a secret and charming bolt hole.

A few of the owner's collection of contemporary English paintings in an intimate corner of the studio/drawing room. The desk is English.

Another detail of the same room.

Opposite, the master bedroom has a hand-painted wallpaper designed especially for the room.

The elegant spare room in this tiny house has taffeta hangings against a hand-painted wallpaper.

The bathroom is outfitted with a combination of faux and real marble.

At the top of the stairs, a dramatically situated 40-inch high French statue.

An Artists' Flat in a Norman Shaw House

*C*arlos Sancha, originally from Spain, comes from a family of artists, whose works are dotted around his London flat. He is himself a well-known portrait painter who specializes in commissions. He is also a considerable muralist, and his wife, Sheila Sancha, is the author and illustrator of delightful children's books devoted to medieval social life.

The flat is a conversion in an extraordinary house which was built by Norman Shaw in 1885 for Marcus Stone, R.A. The present changes were made in 1948, and the Sanchas have lived here for thirty years. Much of the architectural detail has been added by Carlos in do-it-yourself fashion, and he and Sheila are both addicted collectors of memorabilia.

The family portrait by Carlos Sancha was painted in the mid-1970s and is framed in the Florentine style.

The dining hallway. A pastiche in classical style by Carlos Sancha hangs over a serving table which was made from the top of a chimney-piece with banisters for legs. The brass chandelier is Dutch, the dining table and chairs English.

In the drawing room the 18th-century desk stands next to a marble-ized niche housing plants and a 19th-century statue.

A clock barometer bought for £8 on a small satinwood commode.

In the massive hallway, the Broadwood lacquered piano was made originally for the Russian market. The Sancha portrait is of his son in fancy dress at the age of 11; the subject is derived from the famous Victorian painting "When Did You Last See Your Father?" The other objects in the room represent the owners' varied tastes and were collected over many years.

An Art Nouveau bronze urn on a tripod stand.

A "do-it-yourself" enthusiast, Sancha found this elaborate architrave to set around the door leading to the bathroom.

The small conservatory, which is entered through the studio, also serves as an alternative dining area.

In the master bedroom, a group of illustrations by Sheila Sancha for her book *The Luttrell Village*. The looking-glass is Regency, and the fourposter bed is covered with an old English quilt. There are Dutch tiles around the original fireplace which was cut down to scale when the house was converted into apartments.

In the bathroom the Sanchas have created an imaginative dressing-table which conceals the washing machine.

The attic storeroom was originally part of the studio and has huge soaring windows.

Sheila's illustrations for Shell BP were called "Fanta" and appeared monthly in the national newspapers some years ago.

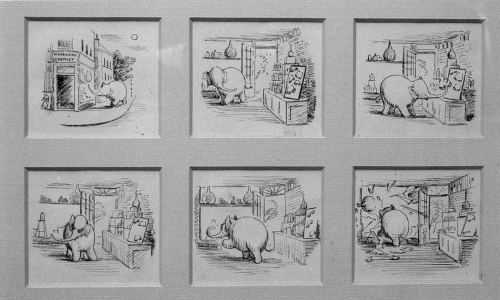

Opposite, the drawings in the studio are by Carlos Sancha's artist father. The painting is by Sancha of his father-in-law.

Royal Avenue in Chelsea is a wide, stately, quiet street that forms, in effect, a square. The terraces of houses on each side are early 19th-century, elegant and large. The film called *The Servant* took place in one of these houses.

A Country Cottage in South Kensington

This double-fronted Victorian cottage, set back in its own garden with a picket fence, is an example of how the countryside still seems every now and then to be an integral part of London. The house is owned by two antique dealers who specialize in rather formal and beautiful furniture. The house they decided to live in, which had in fact remained empty for several years before they finally bought it, is a delight and in sharp contrast to what one might have expected them to choose. The interior provides a joyful surprise, being filled with bibelots, old fabrics vying with new, and an atmosphere of ordered, nostalgic clutter.
A reassuring air of the past pervades both the house and the walled back-garden, which abounds in old-fashioned shrubs and cosy corners to sit in.

Left, the front of the house as seen from the street.

An unusual collection of ivory boxes.

English embossed and embroidered cushions in an occasional armchair in the dining/sitting room.

The dining/sitting room has an antique embroidered table cloth and rich taffeta curtains. The fireplace, one of a pair in the house, is English Regency of black and white marble.

An English oak side table with a collection of glass decanters and English porcelain.

"Fire dogs" sit in front of an elaborate wrought-iron grate. The fender is Regency.

In the drawing room the convex mirror is Regency gilt wood. The crystal and ormolu candlesticks, as well as the mantelshelf, are also Regency. In the niches on each side of the fireplace are hand-painted papier-mâché trays.

A papier-mâché pig, jokey hat stands and a teddy bear sit on top of a Continental blond wood wardrobe.

Baccarat lights of the 1920s have Edwardian crystal-beaded lampshades and stand on a kidney-shaped dressing table with a satin skirt.

A view from the bathroom into the Colefax & Fowler chintz bedroom. The painting in the foreground is by a French artist who painted covers for *Vogue* in the 1940s.

A corner of the country-house kitchen.

Right, the alcove houses a late 17th-century fruitwood bureau and shelves bearing a varied collection of meat plates and bowls.

Opposite, detail of the collection in the kitchen which includes a children's grocery shop from the 1950s.

Living on the Thames

*D*r Michael Barraclough and his wife,
television producer Jenny Barraclough, bought the
land on which they were to build their dream house in
1970. They started building it themselves in 1975 and
the bulk of it was finished after three years; but they
have continued ever since to improve and add to it.
Dr Barraclough built two homes for himself in India
and has been unable since then "to live in other men's
houses". He loves the river and cannot bear to be
hemmed in – hence the courtyards and extensive
view from every level of the house.
Greenwich in all its splendour is just across the river –
a view that the owners want to share with those who
lived in the area before the East London property
boom. They have helped to create collectives to buy
land and share building costs by pooling skills as well
as money.

The house is completely dominated by its vistas and was
built with that in mind.

This angle gives an idea of the house's complex open plan. From the sitting room there is a wide uninterrupted view of the Thames.

Overleaf, comfortable canvas chairs in the dining room. The hanging lampshade is strictly 1960s.

A view from a small sitting room onto one of the numerous metal terraces.

The splendid 17th-century buildings of Greenwich can be seen across the river.

57

A walkway on the bedroom floor with huge windows looking out at the constant activity on the river.

A secluded sitting area for private contemplation.

Garden-like pathways within the house give a glimpse of the back garden.

The River Thames is an integral part of London, crossed by many Londoners twice a day at least. Albert Bridge, a good example of elaborate Victorian engineering and design, provides access between Chelsea and Battersea, with its extensive and much-used Park. When lit up at night, the Bridge takes on an unexpected beauty.

South of the River

The garden of the late 1870s house seen on a summer's day.

Stephen Buckley is a painter of some repute in the contemporary art world. He lives with his wife and two children in Clapham, South London, in a terrace house which, when they bought it, was in a sorry state. Over the years they have added a conservatory kitchen and created a studio for Stephen in the basement.

The character of the house is dictated by their own special style, Stephen's furniture, and their collections of objets trouvés – like the candlesticks on the mantel-piece, among which are products of the Arts and Crafts Movement by Mackintosh and Liberty. The decor is predominantly black and white, and there are naturally a number of Buckleys on the walls.

Trestles look like sculpture in Stephen Buckley's studio.

Overleaf, a view of the drawing room with white slip-covered sofas near the tall bow window. The chair is Lloyd loom basketwork, and the picture on the left-hand wall is by Buckley.

A collection of candlesticks on the dining room mantelshelf includes examples of Liberty, Mackintosh, turn-of-the-century German pewter, and the triangular pair at the rear are by a modern Swiss sculptor.

The dining chairs were being thrown out by friends because of their broken cane-work. Stephen rescued them, covered them in canvas and painted them.

Extended Space within a Mews House

The house has a white stuccoed exterior, such as one has come to expect in most Belgravia streets. In a sense it is simply a mews house, situated as it is on the corner of a typical mews with its cobbled street, but the space inside, with a series of inner courtyards, has a certain amplitude.

Opposite, in the calm, spare hallway hangs a painting by the contemporary German artist Meckseper. The staircase panelling is *faux bois* painted by John Sumter, who did all the specialist painting throughout the house.

Overleaf, the dining room has a *trompe l'oeil* balustrade dado, and the walls are painted to resemble lacquered parchment. The crystal chandelier is 19th-century Swedish. The chairs are 18th-century English in the Chippendale style, upholstered in checked French cotton.

A detail of the paint work in the dining room.

A view of the entrance hall, looking into the dining room. The floor is paved with Brittany stone. All the upholstery and curtains are in *pomme de pins* fabric from Claremont. The desk is 18th-century English burwood, with a Kandinsky painting of 1908 above it. The drawing on the left is by Edward Burra.

One's first impression is of a cool interior in which white and cream predominate. Colour is created by the owner's contemporary picture collection and flowers which are always present in abundance. The house is usually full of people but retains its private domains, as each floor is complete in itself, with separate sitting-rooms for entertaining, reading, children, and even for the dogs behind the kitchen.
This illustrates how often London houses offer an anonymous façade, and yet are individual, intimate and homely inside.

A Léger painting over an early Regency double-sided bookcase.

A Ben Nicholson painting in the drawing room contrasts with a lush bowl of lilies.

The drawing room gives onto a patio with elaborate trellis-work. The owner deliberately chose a range of pale colours in order to create a sense of continuity on the ground floor.

One of a pair of painted Victorian washstands with a Picasso etching from the Vollard Suite.

Right, the red library with a sofa covered in a Claremont cotton. The painting is by Allen Jones.

A view through to the master bathroom from the library.

Two views of a bookcase with a secret door.

In the white marble bathroom there are armchairs covered in striped mattress ticking to create a cosy sitting area.

The bedroom, with chintz and silk, has a traditional and sumptuous atmosphere.

A decorated wastepaper bin in the bathroom.

Left, the walls of the library in this apartment are adorned with a Fortuny fabric, and the baize-covered table serves as a desk.

Above, the façade of Albany which is set back from busy Piccadilly.

A Stone's Throw from Piccadilly Circus

Albany, situated discreetly off Piccadilly next to the Royal Academy, was built in the mid-eighteenth century and has been the address of many famous people. Behind the main building, stone entrance halls lead off a covered walkway which leads to Old Burlington Street. Nothing in the original structure has changed; only the private apartments with their varied interiors hint of the late twentieth century.

The owner of this apartment acquired it fifteen years ago, and with the help of the American decorator Malcolm Bancroft was able to design a comfortable and stylish home.

Right, the drawing room, its walls also covered with Fortuny, has a French mirror facing its pair in the library. The screen was especially painted for the apartment.

Below, Chinese late 18th-century figurines are arrayed in front of a Biedermeier clock.

This Chinese lacquer cabinet has a pair of Chinese birds on the top flanking a porcelain dish.

Overleaf, the bedroom leads to an extravagantly mirrored bathroom hung with a Victorian Gypsy mirror. The walls of the bedroom are covered with fabric.

In the entrance hall there is a compact, hidden kitchen behind the row of cupboards.

The plates are part of a service that belonged to Lady Hamilton.

In Cadogan Square, which lies on the very border between Chelsea and Belgravia, the prevailing tall brick buildings, now almost all of them converted into expensive, capacious apartments with high ceilings, were dubbed "Pont Street Dutch" by Osbert Lancaster. Built in the 1870s and '80s, their most distinctive features are their terracotta gables and heavy decoration.

The quiet cul-de-sac is in the heart of busy Chelsea.

A view from the dining room looking towards the conservatory/sitting room. The dinner plates and bowls are American sponge ware, the candlesticks English late 19th-century. Above the painted cupboard is a still-life by the 1930s artist Merinsky.

Two Minutes from the King's Road

Situated at the end of a cul-de-sac in a Chelsea backwater is a three-storey double-fronted house. Occupying the whole of the ground floor, with its conservatory and small walled garden, live an artist and his interior-designer wife. The rooms are small, but there is an illusion of space, as each room leads off the next. The owners say, "Sometimes we have to remember that this is a flat and not a house. The bonus of a sitting-room converted from a rather miserable conservatory, and the garden which we cram with as many flowers as the small space will allow, make it hard for us to believe we could ever replace it anywhere else."
Pictures are hung wherever there is wall space. There are subtle colour combinations, an interplay of patterns, and a real sense of domestic comfort.

Right top, a French table clock is hung between windows decorated with cream glazed-cotton festoon curtains. On the table among the blue and white porcelain is a small bronze dancer by Allen Jones.

Right centre, a collection of Leeds creamware is displayed on a Victorian inlaid table. Harry, the West Highland terrier, sits below a Matthew Smith drawing.

Right bottom, the Provençal commode bears an arrangement of pottery bowls by Karen Bunting. The sculptures are by Elisabeth Frink and John Davies.

Opposite, in the library the sofa is covered in a Colefax & Fowler print. The tulip-shaped table lamp was bought new by the owner's great-aunt in the early 1930s at the London furniture shop Maple's. The set of anemone prints are by Bill Jacklin.

Above, the sofa and chair in the drawing room are slip-covered in French mattress ticking. The pictures are by Bomberg, Merinsky and Epstein. Flanked by bronze candlesticks and a pair of cloisonné birds, the gilded mirror over the mantel-piece is 18th-century French.

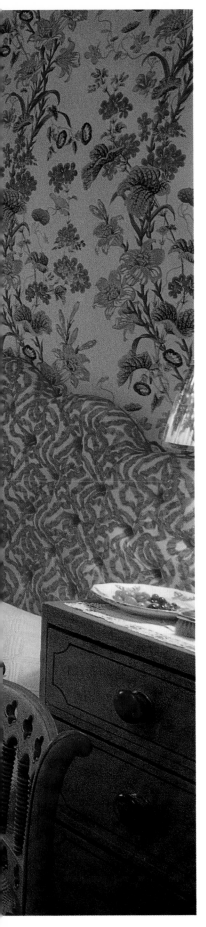

The bedroom, with its "Lilies and Geranium" wall covering by Colefax & Fowler, echoes the garden beyond. On the wall are a black and white print by Bill Jacklin and two linocuts by Claude Flight.

On the bedside chest of drawers is the owner's blue enamel dressing-table set and her own childhood radio from 1953.

Overleaf, the conservatory/sitting room existed when the present owner moved into the flat, but heating and bookcases were installed to create warmth, and the walls were painted a soft pink colour. The rug is American and adds a rakish touch to the English chintz and the carpet armchair. The rattan blinds are always drawn as the room faces south.

An Architect Builds His Own Dream House

The well-known contemporary architect Richard Burton has fulfilled a dream to build his own house in the middle of London.
One enters through a secret door set in a wall in a fairly anonymous street. Within, there has been erected a unique glass roof and garden. Much of the work was done by the owner himself and still continues – a studio is being built at present – but already the garden is mature, and an exciting project has been brought to fruition.

Above, the painted metal gate at the entrance to the house in North London gives no hint of what lies beyond.

Right, the opened gate shows the covered walkway behind. The house is to the right of the path.

The garden to the left of the paved
walkway. The hole in the back
wall echoes the entrance door at
the street end.

The house revolves around the kitchen/dining room which is decorated with an antique kilim.

Above right, a small still-life is created in the bedroom.

Far right, a small carved wooden French model of a pulpit.

Right, a small choice collection of memorabilia set into the kitchen wall.

Overleaf, the classical-style terraces designed by John Nash in Regent's Park in the first quarter of the 19th century form some of the noblest and grandest habitations in London. Elaborately fashioned to resemble palaces, they represented an ambitious monument to a thriving city. Now they provide handsome apartments, with some of the most spectacular park views London can offer.

99

Living in a Nash Terrace House

The hall has faux stone walls and specially built pillars to create the effect of a courtyard.

*T*he terraces designed by Nash in 1812-25 to describe a virtual circle around Regent's Park are more varied than they seem at first sight. All of them, however, have the virtue of affording exquisite views of one of London's most handsome parks.

The owner of this house has lived here for many years and had the classic decorating firm of Colefax and Fowler to help in the task of restoring the interiors. Over the years the decor has mellowed, and it has been enhanced by a vast collection of Leeds china, which is crammed on shelves wherever one looks.

A view through to the drawing room.

An 18th-century English lacquer commode with a collection of 18th-century Leeds ware. The pair of birds are 17th-century Chinese.

In the drawing room a magnificent Chinese Chippendale mirror hangs over the mantelshelf. The walls are covered with a citrus-yellow silk and the curtains are made of checked taffeta. The interior design was executed by Tom Parr of Colefax & Fowler over twenty years ago and has hardly needed to be touched since.

The floor of the dining room is a painted chequerboard. The Regency English dining chairs are also painted.

Part of the owners' large collection of 18th-century Leeds creamware.

A view into the library from the dining room.

The doors in the library are false
bookcases and lead into the
dining room. The carpet is
Bessarabian and the octagonal
table in the foreground is English
painted in the Egyptian style.

A view of the garden with the family spaniel.

Every year in this Central London garden the beekeeper extracts honey from the hives on the front lawn.

The garden has cobbled sitting areas.

Overleaf, the terraces of North London are composed of smaller, narrower houses, taking on the characteristics of larger houses built in an earlier period. They sport bow windows and have heavily decorated stucco facades. Many of these streets are associated with media personalities; seriously successful, politically committed men and women who wield forceful pens, word processors, cameras and microphones.

Surprises in West London

The modest exterior of Nelson Morrow's maisonette in Shepherd's Bush.

Opposite, the roof garden is a few steps down from the bedroom and faces the backs of a terrace of Victorian houses.

Overleaf: top, a table has been created from 1930s painters' trestles. The top is M.D.F. board and the whole thing was sprayed with car paint. The chairs are covered in a classic Colefax & Fowler linen.

Below, left, Nelson Morrow designed this portable bookcase in a blond wood. The original was made for a Scottish library and the model was found in a junk shop.

Below, right, an inlaid marquetry table of the 19th century, with Victorian boxes and photographs.

Opposite, the well-proportioned drawing room. On the mantelshelf is a collection of Grand Tour bronzes. The Portuguese needlework rug is a Morrow Reis design adapted from a 19th-century carpet. A stool doubles as a coffee table and is covered with a modern reproduction of a paisley shawl. The cover on the circular table with its collection of memorabilia is a Victorian wool fabric.

*N*elson Morrow, of the decorating firm Morrow Reis Designs, has created the most delightful and imaginative maisonette (or duplex) at the top of a modest terrace house in Shepherd's Bush. As he was able to buy only one floor, he was left with no space for a bedroom. He therefore raised the roof to make another floor, and built a terrace outside the new bedroom and compact bathroom.
The flat has Morrow's special touches: sofas wrapped in rugs, meticulous tablescapes, lots of old fabrics, good lighting.
The ordinary house in an ordinary street gives very little away from the outside, but inside it is full of surprises.

The sofa is covered with a tartan rug and skirted in a 19th-century fabric. The cushions are made up from the owner's collection of fabrics and consist of Indian scarves, paisleys and old Portuguese cottons.

Opposite, above the desk in the study is a drawing of one of the Morrow Reis designs.

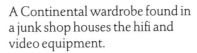

A Continental wardrobe found in a junk shop houses the hifi and video equipment.

A collection of 19th-century drawings of Spain are reflected in the simple mirror in the study.

Left, a view from the bedroom towards the roof terrace. The chest of drawers and the chair are English. The two drawings next to the bathroom door are by Bakst.

The simple black and white bathroom has an Amtico floor that creates a 3-D effect.

More Bakst drawings over the bed which is covered with a Morrow Reis fabric, "Gloria".

The lower half of Tite Street, leading down to the River bank, is famous for Oscar Wilde's residence and for the artists (such as Whistler and Sargent) who had specially built studios here in the late 19th century. A row of highly individual, mostly brick buildings with eccentric features, they have outlasted their original intentions.

Chelsea
Traditional

The floor of the gracious hallway is marble. The French mantelpiece is also marble and carries a collection of painted candlesticks. On the English console are a pair of Japanese figures.

A large wooden monkey stands guard in the hallway.

*This magnificent house in the heart of Chelsea
was built for a prosperous artist at the end of the
nineteenth century. Its main feature is the huge studio
which dominates half the house. The present owners
put in a galleried library to add shape to the room,
and elaborate curtains to help to accentuate the sheer
height of the windows. The bedroom, with a double-
height ceiling, was also added more recently.
The addition of a Japanese contemplation room and
bathroom was put into the hands of Japanese
builders. The garden too was designed in the
Japanese manner, and its tranquillity makes it hard
to believe that the King's Road, with its boutiques
and throngs of bright young people, is just around
the corner.*

The vast drawing room has elaborate curtains which
complement the scale of the windows. The silk sofas,
candles and soft lighting create a decorative and
seductive atmosphere.

The deep comfortable sofa has a colourful collection of cushions covered in old fabrics.

An Indian horse prances on the kilim carpet that is spread over the richly carved side table.

The drawing room as seen from the galleried library.

Far left, a doorway from the drawing room leads out to the Japanese quarters.

Left, the Zen garden.

Below, the bathroom with its wooden tub was built by Japanese craftsmen and is completely authentic.

Opposite, the Japanese meditation room leading out to the Zen garden.

The bedroom is double-height and has a raftered ceiling. It was built at a later date than the rest of the house.

The large master bathroom has a wooden floor and panelling combined with an old-fashioned hotel-type marble bath.

Overleaf, Little Venice: a totally unexpected oasis of bosky charm not far at all from central London. Along the banks are broad, light-hearted stucco villas, many with large gardens. That perennial and ageless beauty, Diana Duff Cooper, lived here in her later years, and Robert Browning had a house quite close to the Canal.

Brocades and Marbling off Hyde Park

*T*his house, situated in an unassuming street on the "wrong" (that is, north) side of Hyde Park, has a gracious exterior and very high ceilings.
An art dealer and collector has created a rich, formal background for his wonderfully eclectic collection of contemporary paintings and drawings. The walls are either boldly covered with vibrant brocades or painted with elaborate finishes, and it is interesting that neither treatment detracts in the least from the art which is always being added to in exciting ways.

Opposite, the painted hallway with faux stonework; the carpet is a Ferouz runner.

Three different paint treatments.

Above, the façade and front door are typical of houses in this area near Marble Arch.

The drawing room is decorated with a Fortuny wall-cover and curtains. Above the chimney-piece is a classical *capriccio* by Woolton.

Above, a Woolton landscape hangs above the George III gilt wood sofa covered with brocade.

Below, a view of the narrow end of the drawing room. The painting on the easel is by Leon Kossoff. The walls are covered with fabric.

In the tented downstairs lavatory
there is a plaster cast of a relief
from the Athens Parthenon
below the dado.

A portrait by Frank Auerbach above a Regency sofa in the library.

A George II mahogany card-table stands next to a window in the drawing room.

Left, the small breakfast room, with a painting by Bill Jacklin.

A Flemish carved Pietà.

The terrace in winter.

The Victorian façade of the block of flats and (*left*) the view of the Earl's Court Exhibition Centre that can be seen from the main windows of John Wright's flat.

John Wright, an eminent interior designer-architect, has transformed a late Victorian mansion flat in Earl's Court into a background of his own vision.
The structural changes are evident, and several rooms have been swapped around to create the right flow. Vistas have been opened up between rooms by the use of columns and double doors. These columns are used again in the hall to dramatize the space, and lighting plays an important role in creating a unique atmosphere – both modern and classical.

143

In the hallway looking towards the front door is a 19th-century plaster cast of an ancient Egyptian head. The curtain covering the door was designed by Carolyn Quartermaine.

The console in the front lobby was made in the 1940s. On the left is a piece of plaster cornice designed by John Wright for a client. The etching is one of a series on fireplaces printed in the 1920s.

The sofa in the drawing room was designed by the owner. In the corner by the Le Corbusier chair stands a Danish torchère of about 1800. The large charcoal drawing is by Alison Lambert.

Below, a 1930s table with glass legs; the top is made of bird's-eye maple. The terracotta urn is Swedish (1800). The Grand Tour *objets* are of bronze and marble.

Opposite, a plaster bust stands in the grate of a cast iron fireplace. The vases on the mantelshelf are of alabaster and terracotta in the Egyptian style. The drawing is by Ricardo Cinalli.

ohn Wright's interpretation of neo-classical design is individual. He uses neutral colour to help one enjoy the forms of the furniture, the collected objects and pictures. Each room differs and was inspired by different influences, such as Arts and Crafts in the study and Josef Hoffmann in one of the bathrooms.

The bookshelves in the dining room/library were designed by John Wright expressly for the room and were influenced by Sir John Soane's work. The Napoleonic engravings on the wall are of Egyptian temples. The metal structure on the left is a copy of a Pompeian tripod, and the dining chair is 1950s Italian. The hanging lamp is alabaster, 1920s. The intriguing archway between the dining and drawing rooms was specially designed by John Wright.

Looking into the drawing room from the dining room. The drawings are by Margaret Priest and the dinner plates were designed by Jean Cocteau.

A study cupboard designed by
John Wright is described as a cross
between Biedermeier and
Japanese.

In the warmly coloured study with its striped wallpaper,
a shawl is thrown over the sofa. The pictures are mostly
English, between 1900 and 1940. On the terracotta
painted mantelshelf is a group of Japanese vases.

The master bathroom, situated opposite the bedroom, has granite tiles.

On the walls of the guest bathroom are a set of Dutch Art Nouveau furniture designs. The black and white tiles lend a touch of Josef Hoffmann's style.

Previous pages, at one end of the hallway in this top-floor flat, an 18th-century Buddha stands beneath a small model of a North African arched portico. In the foreground, a plaster cast of a Greek warrior adds a dramatic accent.

A glimpse of the main bedroom from the hall. The cotton window panels were designed by Carolyn Quartermaine.

The blue bedroom has a collection of views of India by William Daniels (*c.* 1800). The chair is 17th-century Indo-Dutch. On each side of the bed, small Moroccan tables are used for the simple wooden reading lamps.

Overleaf, Pelham Crescent is one of the gems of South Kensington: a curved row of restrained façades with decorative ironwork, protected by trees from the rumble of Fulham Road traffic.

A Palatial Folly

The graceful and modest front of the house, which was formerly an artist's studio and was rebuilt in 1985.

The design of this Italianate castle, unlike any other house in London, was a collaboration between the owner, Mr Frank Lowe, his wife Michelle, David Bristow and Keith Priest. Each person made a special contribution in different areas, but all worked together to create the overall design. Once in the central courtyard, one can easily imagine oneself in Tuscany. Its "Romeo and Juliet" staircase leads up to an extraordinary roof garden, which affords a vast panorama of London – a unique combination.
The house was originally a photographic studio and was completely rebuilt in the Continental style.

The floor of the entrance way is covered with French tiles.

Left, the three-storey hallway has a pronounced Mediterranean atmosphere.

Below, this fountain was discovered by Mr Lowe in Paris.

Right, the enormous skylight at the top of the house.

The tiles in the kitchen were made in Makuum, Holland. The farmyard mural is based on traditional Dutch tiling designs from the factory in Makuum.

Another view of the kitchen with its Dutch tiles and large scrubbed pine table.

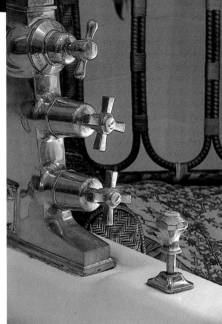

The bathroom tiles were designed and made in Wales.

In a small sitting room decorated in the French manner, the mural was painted by Jean Harris.

The marble chimney-piece in the study came from Macon in France.

The drawing room has a Biedermeier table and chairs. The furniture is mostly Continental and the floor is covered with rush matting. The ceiling is slightly domed and the room, leading off the hall, has no window of its own.

The lighting in the billiards room
was designed by David Bristow.

Right, the nursery has murals by Jean Bristow.

Below, the downstairs washroom.

Right, the rooftop eyrie with its view down Glebe Place towards the King's Road.

Overleaf, the rooftop garden was designed by Frank Lowe and David Bristow.

Right, the Italian fountain was found at the Antiquaires du Louvre in Paris.

One of London's countless
private gardens – this one hidden
away in the heart of fashionable
Kensington.

In the heart of the East End of London, long known as a working-class quarter, there is a street of back-to-back terrace cottages which has hardly changed over the years. Most of it is owned by a Trust and lived in by artists.

In one of these cottages, the painter Peter Bunting and his potter wife Karen have fashioned an atmosphere all their own. Their work is everywhere to be seen, along with all sorts of memorabilia they have picked up here and there for very little money and put together with great flair.

A back view of the Buntings' East End house.

A little pool with a monster in the back garden.

Opposite, a painting by Peter Bunting lies finished on the studio floor.

Artists with a Lot of Style

Stacked paintings on one side of the studio.

The well-lit studio with works in progress.

Overleaf, a view of the sitting room with a selection of very personal memorabilia. The paintings are by Peter Bunting.

Top right, a group of *objets trouvés* displayed in the sitting room.

Below right, the Edwardian upright piano just fits into a corner of the sitting room. The lamp is an example of Arts and Crafts leaded glass.

181

Karen Bunting is a well-known potter; all the pieces on display are used in daily life.

Karen's kiln and more examples of her work.

183

A Remodelled Eighteenth-Century Vicarage

Opposite: the spacious garden behind the house with period details.

*C*anonbury House was built in 1765. Originally a vicarage and not considered in any way a grand manor house, it was erected on the site of the old Tower of Canonbury, which went back to 1509.

The present owner bought the house twelve years ago as a derelict rooming house which had stood empty for five years. He has restored it to its former glory, removing the Victorian and Edwardian accretions, and making it fit for modern living with a basement converted into a kitchen and its offices, plus a rather imposing dining-room. Now in its full splendour, an oasis of peace and quiet in a heavily populated area, the house and its ample grounds combine a feeling of elegance and comfort.

The drawing room is formal but eminently comfortable. On the chimney-piece, a pair of granite obelisks, two gilt 17th-century pieces and a Greek urn are only a small sample of the extensive collection of memorabilia in the house.

In the small sitting area at the garden end of the drawing room, a backgammon table stands next to the window. The china pots on the window sill are German. An ebony figure from the Ivory Coast stands next to a Continental commode in the drawing room.

The inner hallway. The console table is Swedish
Biedermeier. The abstract painting on the stairs is by the
English artist Derek Hirst.

The walls of the basement dining room are covered with
an American vinyl to resemble tortoise-shell. The
painting is a posthumous portrait of a boy of five (1595).
The painting over the marble inlaid serving table is of
Suffolk by John O'Connor.

In the morning room are a set of family photographs in silver frames. The paintings are by Lorri, an Australian painter living in Rome.

Right, above a chiffonier-bookcase in the morning room is a collection of French and English Impressionists.

Far right, bronze figures on a small fruitwood table.

A painting by Kevin Pearsh over the French chimney-piece. The bronze clock is French.

A Comfortable House in North London

A typical street of Victorian working-class cottages in Kentish Town.

*B*arbara Broun is one of London's foremost paint specialists and muralists. In her own house in Kentish Town, however, her particular brand of decorating is hardly in evidence. She bought the run-down house over seven years ago and is still working on it. She says this is because she has been just too busy doing other people's houses, and also because she has become rather fond of plain white paint.

Until recently, one of the rooms housed a ghost whose presence was marked by an overwhelming female scent. Barbara was unable to use the room, and only after a very strong-smelling varnish was used on the floor did the perfume disappear.

For all its smallness, the house boasts high ceilings and a pleasing squareness. Ghost or not, it is a comfortable, stylish home in an area of Victorian terrace houses built around the railway lines.

The hallway has a Turkey carpet and simple painted walls above a faux wood painted dado.

Two views of the small sitting room with its unusually high ceiling. The sofa and chairs are covered with a wool tartan.

The painted effect on the mantel-piece in the sitting room was achieved by soaking the surface in a form of acid.

Overleaf, a view through the pristine white kitchen and the garden beyond.

A corner of the bathroom. Old stained glass doors are used to make a wall and architectural interest in a tiny room.

The dining room is hung with paintings by a neighbour of the owner.

Above, the mantel-piece in the studio has been painted to look like porphyry. The objects placed so artfully on the shelf are of no monetary value.

Right, the studio – formerly haunted – is now used and enjoyed.

Lord North Street, with its dignified 18th-century
houses, has been a haunt of Members of Parliament,
since it is close to the Palace of Westminster. A short,
one-block street, it leads to Smith Square, which is
dominated by St John's Church, a Baroque edifice now
deconsecrated and used as a concert hall.

200

A Garden Studio

A view from the drawing room into the secluded garden. The door is flanked by a child's chair and a light-hearted collection of hats.

The garden, looking towards the house. Sarah McAlpine collaborated with Clifton Nurseries to create the garden.

In the second walled garden, a mirror seems to promise a third.

Sarah McAlpine's studio, which stands at the end of her garden, was one of several rebuilt in the mid-1950s on the site of those that belonged originally to Chelsea Art School.
The garden was redesigned only recently, the idea being to create secret gardens leading from one to another and helped by the use of mirrors to suggest yet a third garden.
The studio is pure theatre and is used mainly in the evenings for entertaining. Aubergine walls, animal printed fabrics and wall sculptures by Kenneth Turner contribute to the impression of a stage setting.

A detail of the black painted bookcase on the stairs.

The main hall of the house, which was built in the 1950s, doubles as an occasional dining room. The mirror creates the effect of a much larger space.

The rich foliage in the garden has only been planted since 1984.

The small pool with its water-spouting god's head hidden away in the first garden.

Opposite: the doors into the studio/sitting room which provides an ideal venue for entertaining at night.

A corner of the studio with a
bridge table and chinoiserie chairs
painted by Sarah McAlpine.

The elaborate wall sculptures are
by Ken Turner and act as light
sources as well as mirrors.

The studio has an eclectic
collection of furniture, pictures
and fabrics. Against the aubergine
walls they work together to give
the large room an enjoyable
atmosphere like that of a tasteful
nightclub.

A Flat of the Thirties

$\mathscr{S}$wan Court, a pre-war block of flats that used to boast its own restaurant, still gives one the feeling of walking into the past. When it was built in 1932, artists' studios were incorporated on the top storey with views towards the river.

The view from the living room of this Swan Court flat is across Chelsea to the Thames. Although it cannot qualify as a beautiful panorama, it is a characteristic London scene.

Inset, the vase holding an ice plant in the bathroom is Poole 1925.

𝒯n this flat, interior designer Hugh Leslie has managed with a minimum of redecoration to retain the original feel of the building. A magnificent Gluck painting with its Lalique frame dominates the studio/drawing-room which is sparsely but comfortably furnished to emphasize the space.

Alvara Guevara painted the six pictures above the Le Corbusier sofa. Guevara considered himself English and was a great friend of that Twenties personality, Nancy Cunard.

The bronze head is the work of Glyn Philpot in the late 1920s.

The Gluck painting with its Lalique frame takes pride of place in the double-height living room. The dining chairs are by Philippe Starck and the glass-and-chrome side table is an Eileen Gray design. The side table is by Edwin Lutyens and is one of six made for the Viceroy's residence in Delhi.

An Apartment in Docklands

*R*ae Hoffenberg is a designer and property developer. She was one of the pioneers in Docklands to get abandoned warehouses authorized for residential use and then convert them into desirable houses and flats. She has also fought for the local population to live in improved conditions and not to be forced out of the area.

Her own apartment is open-plan, creating its own spaces by the use of indoor plants and screens. There is a conservatory feeling about the space, and she has managed to bring the outside with its magnificent views into the flat, thus creating a unique and personal environment. The decor is kept to a minimum, but with Rae Hoffenberg's extensive collection of objets, interior decoration is hardly necessary.

Previous page, the simple façade of the house in Docklands and the main living room has exposed brick walls and a vast collection of house plants, which profit from the skylight built into the beamed ceiling.

A row of converted warehouses in East London. The centre section was all rebuilt by Rae Hoffenberg.

Redevelopment of the area in progress.

Panoramic view of the Thames from Rae Hoffenberg's apartment.

The brick walls in this soaring room complement the owner's extensive collection of paintings.

An African sculpture amid a group of memorabilia.

A view from the bedroom into the dining area of the large living area.

Horn and silver beakers on a table covered with a varied collection of boxes.

The dining table with English silver place settings.

Overleaf, Chiswick Mall, which has remained almost unchanged since the 19th century, illustrates yet another facet of London's infinite variety.

Index